FLYING BENEATH THE DOG STAR:

POEMS FROM A PANDEMIC

poems by

Kathryn Winograd

Finishing Line Press
Georgetown, Kentucky

FLYING BENEATH THE DOG STAR:

POEMS FROM A PANDEMIC

ACKNOWLEDGMENTS

The Colorado Sun: Waking After the Pink Moon and Eighteen Hundred
Dead, April 15, 2020
Kingsview & Co Website: To the Three Ducks Flying Beneath The Dog Star,
October 17, 2020
Red Earth Ink Anthology: Creation and the Cosmos: A Poetic Anthology
Inspired by Nature (March 2021): Small as Rain, Morning on a Cabin Porch,
To the Three Ducks Flying Beneath the Dog Star, Snow on Good Friday, To
the Swallow This Spring at the Nest Box
Tiny Seed Literary Journal: To the Swallow This Spring at the State Park's
Nest Box, October 11, 2020

Publisher: Leah Huete de Maines
Editor: Christen Kincaid
Cover Art: Kathryn Winograd
Author Photo: Cassandra Vagher
Cover Design: Mary Tostanoski

Order online: www.finishinglinepress.com
also available on amazon.com

Author inquiries and mail orders:
Finishing Line Press
PO Box 1626
Georgetown, Kentucky 40324
USA

Table of Contents

to my sister
to all of us lonely

. . . an instrument for the god, who directs their
movements, their calls or cries, and their
formations which are sometimes contrary,
sometimes favouring, as winds are;

on the divination of birds,
Plutarch, De sollertia animalium 975 A

The earth wants to rise; it wants
sun warmth and bird shadow;
it wants our hands breaking the small
nuggets of winter, cold and dark
at the center, maybe a tiny thread,
maybe something we don't know
the name for, rooting deeper . . .

To the Three Ducks Flying Beneath the Dog Star

So little you know, wild-winged
and unshaken beneath a dog star,
half-grazing the pines, the bare winter
aspen I stand in the dark wash of
waiting for the tip of a yellow moon.
In Ohio, girlhood, these April stars
circled a pond bull-dozed
by my father, a raft of cattail
where the red-wings spun their nests
above the scrim of caught water.
Tonight, in this near dark, so close
my hand could circle it,
Sirius hovers above the red
factory lights of Pueblo
and the Sangre de Cristos
blue-washed in this hour.
I am cold in this wind,
in this spine of the Milky Way,
these blue white stars named
for a bear or a lyre or a woman
weeping her dead into a river.
I think I was still half-sleeping
in a field of grass, in a haze
of stars, in a far and nameless
country you care nothing
about, burying and unburying
those I love. Such quiet,
the mining trucks to the north
stalled and the little generator
of a shed where no one lives
in winter shut down.
And then, your wings,
almost, against the moon.
Why must I always be alone,
searching for something beautiful?

Waking after the Pink Moon and Eighteen Hundred Dead

Prayer began early
before the sterling jays
dove, then clattered at our window,
flicked the blue dark
storm of their tails.
Our pale trees bow down
and a nuthatch teeters upside down
from the birdfeeder post I buried
with stones another spring,
his fine beak tapping
at the seed I left out all night.
My breath, how lightly it floats
in this chill spring like a delicate
frost of air I can walk through.
I take the wood axe from our tool
shed to split the old wood
we felled and stacked years past.
Last night, I stood alone
in the deepening dusk,
in the silence, as if I could rename
each splinter of star I did not know.
And then the pink moon soft
as the fingertips of the dead
slid over the mountain and I lit
fires beneath a moon of far
blossoms. How long ago,
it seems, springs when we could just
count the catkin on the budding
aspen and step so carefully
through the winter grass
so as not to crush the white globes
of the wind flowers lifting themselves
from the cold earth.

Rescuing a Junco Stunned by our Window

Two days our windows
mirrored winter: metallic
trees with little nothing
knots of ghost buds
and snow leaves, finches
as if lacquered on ancient tintype,
the clouds silver-washed
as if to lure the wild
birds to our unbroken glass.
We half-guessed before
these solitary days what
sometimes happens: a tiny
breast feather I'd find pinned
to a window pane, or a sparrow
or a finch adrift, lopsided
in the yellow cinquefoil.
But I did not know
what bitter cold
and daily seed can bring,
how bird after bird can fire
out of the frosted trees
or from a feeder post I sawed
and nailed in some now
forgotten joy. You said,
"A bombardment," the quick
window thuds it seemed
moments after I poured out
our sunflower seed and then
those stunned and floating wings.

How could I have imagined
one morning scooting
a pole across a snowy porch
roof to flip a bird
past our metal snow
guard and watch it hang
by a toe, a bead of bright
blood, a berry, at the tip
of its beak, before it spilled
backward into the basket you held?
We tucked the little junco
by the stove, sheltered it
with the day's newspaper. It slept,
huddled in a rag, in our same
dark, where it dreamed, I think,
as if we let it go—
unknown to us then what
silences to come, broken
only by the radio's count
of grief and our own dreams
of stellar jays ushering us
through quiet, woken woods.

Divination for My Husband

*Many birds there are that pass to and fro
under the rays of the sun, and not all are fateful*   —*Odyssey*

So necessary, it seemed,
this small concrete bowl
painted green I drove
last spring to settle
outside our wild door,
a tiny reservoir
I filled with well water
for the birds against the summer's
passing dust, the world,
otherwise, too ruinous—
the telescoping of your ill
body we waited for,
as if the surgeon's tool
were an aperture, a light-
gatherer to study
you and your visiting foreign
moons. "So tired of this,"
you said, every pale aspen
we loved—notched black
by antler or bear claw or nuthatch—
a confrontation, then,
what even the bird flutter
unclasped, like an unconsciousness
our watching, a kind of voyeurism,
chickadee and bushtit at the bath's
edge, *little poets*,
I told you, tippling the water.
Surely, the torn sage
I rubbed that spring between
my hands silvered for purpose,
and burns, though unlit, still

sacred, and the stellar jay
that shadows me, yellow-
browed, in my small walks
from you, splinters our ceiling
of sky for reason. This morning
in this strange, new world
where we count the dead daily,
I left but for a moment to fill
my plastic broken jug
at the kitchen sink, still
afraid, and when I returned
bearing, I kept thinking,
my little tomb of water, you,
who can no longer hear the birds,
so heaven-high, so
thin their bells unclappered,
said, *wren*, so happy, you,
in that staccato of descent, this bird
on your knee briefest, lightest.

Finding Snow on Good Friday

The sky, not even bruised,
spills its light, blue
as the petals of the wild iris
wound in their buried boats
beneath the morning fire ash
I throw to the cold wind, again.
I think the iris, named
for a rainbow goddess
of such purity and loved so
by a god, must belong to early
summer, and so it will not
rise yellow-eyed and soon
in my dark harbors of grass
and aspen root no matter
what I dreamed last night
or whom I wept for
or how long I linger in this gold
slip of sun on the porch step.
Maybe tomorrow, in tiny
pockets of earth and worn
granite or in this last snow
that does not drift away,
I will find the pasque-flower.
And quiet and trembling
for its purpled flesh and early
blossom, I will call
it love. And sorrow, too.

The Day that Shook My Faith

I learned the brain can burn
to glass and bones to crystal.
In old Pompei in 70 A.D.,
ash or pumice stone
felled these quiet ones
trapped at the sea, their soft
bodies girdled in stone
for centuries, while others
far off across the Bay
of Naples, it's said,
watched and prayed for death,
for no god they could find.
I am a house fugitive today,
plotting a near dusk heist
in the front garden
along the empty street,
ghostly schoolyard bells
ringing out the hours
and raucous street crows
standing sentry at our birdbath,
washing whatever scrap—
bread, bone—the curbed
trash leaves. This new
world of ours has turned
past the spring equinox,
turned past how many
dead, our celestial equator
unequal in what light
touches now, in what
darkness touches now.
Eternal night,
the onlookers feared,

raining out of the mouth
of Mt Vesuvius
over the shadow bodies
we still find sitting
knees up in vanished
corners, their teeth *perfect*,
our scientists note,
as they scan the pumice casts
where every prayer burst
to flame. Still, I
want to think the earth
does gentle, so for now,
I will bury my boxed potato
buds at the east window
to sun, tuck each bud
into the wire flower stand
between my pink flowers
and their indiscriminate
roots, my succulents
at the window glass green
and bending.

Hanami of Loneliness

I watch the squirrels, plump
with our sunflower seeds,
dangle in the cherry tree
and its blossoms I planted
to block the neighbor's view.
Even the dogs doze
through these squirrels tracking
our old fence tops
and the boughs of a fifty-year old
pine I didn't plant
that each year stretches
across our backyard.
Three linger this morning
in this crooked cherry tree
I pruned wrong too
many years ago
to right or maybe I
underfed or maybe rooted
too deep in manure-burn.
Sometimes, I want to take
the pencil stub I use to write
the grocery list from the kitchen
drawer and crosshatch
the backs of bills and returned
envelopes into something
I fear I'll never see:
cherry blossoms floating
down strange rivers, pink
dawns when I cannot
sleep for counting the dead,
and birds, swallows, I think,
tipped by expressive lines,
by a haze of moon, by
white volcanoes
                    delicate
and touching.

Returning to Phantom Canyon

"You want free wonton
soup?" my Asian friend
at the pickup window asks
through her mask—this tiny
Chinese restaurant she owns
housed in the pink shell
of a Taco Bell, my usual
pit stop. Then I drive
up Rainbow Pass,
down Phantom Canyon,
across the sunken cattle
guard to the bleached porch
steps of our cabin.
The quiet shocks,
all day my goal in this strange
and awful world not to cry.
Just birds now:
bluebird and raven shadow,
light a pale linen
someone has laid out to dry.

Driving Up from the Suburbs

This is not the end, but feels it.
Below, the striped tulip bowls
floated through the night air,
a graffiti of hungry gardens
at my neighbors' doorsteps,
glass shards, those decades-
old coke bottles at the mouth
of our culverts, a dim green.
My tiny mother, who would not
speak to me today, sits in her chair
by her yellow window,
holding her hands.
Once I stood in an English
garden, its cold rain
and birdsong torrent.
A far country, as I see it now,
where unwilded hawks bate
from their tethered thongs, freed
to the wind thermals to stoop
over wet meadows and the half-
leafed woods my mother and I
both yearn for. But, *here*
collects in the white circlets
of first blossoms, even joy
in the three purple-plumed asters
I find in the granite rock,
and in the three spotted horses
bent against the neighbor's hill
above the crooked homestead barn,
and even driving here, alone
and helpless to love enough,
I find joy in a child's lost grey shoe
that someone has hung
on a fencepost, tenderly.

For the Black Angus Sold This Spring

Each winter until, finally,
barely, spring, the black
angus cows returned
to graze the fields we rented
to our neighbor, to drift
through our high mountain meadows
past glory holes and the half-buried
barbed wire a homesteader
nailed a hundred years
ago to the trees. All month,
I have missed them, though
perhaps in the springs past
that we've had of days and days
of solitary jays and the tiny
mouse skulls that I pocket
to hold tenderly in my hand
and show you, this day is still
only the day before the day
of their coming, the day before
they will once again wander
up the ancient paths, their hooves
chipping at the old cow pies
that our dogs, now ash, rolled in.
This spring, I think, far
into mid- summer, I'll wish
for them, for their calves sleeping
mid-day in old winter
grass, tucked so quietly in
as if they were a dark blossoming
before the evening's dream:
the earth returning everything
to us now, perhaps musky
and heavy with its clustered yarrow
and its blue harebells of grief,

but here.

Not Your Light, But Snow Softly

to Stanley Kunitz, The Round

Not your light, but snow softly
this late evening on this yellow
ranch grass bowing earthward
on its brittle stems; and, no,
no blossoms, not like yours,
nothing blue-petaled
the darkness could ebb and flow
down over the hidden pockets
of my sleeping voles and field mice;
tonight I saw late frost
sculpt the pines, cones
in their constant swelling,
my ever-blooming conifers
glossy with pitch and sap.

A stillness softens me.

So I have lit the wood stove of my cabin.
So I have climbed upward to the eaves.
So I am sitting in a cave
of light and knotted wood,
clasping my hands at my desk
with you and your words,
 and your poems to teach me—

and I rest my fingers on my keyboard
and I read you wild and kneeling
in your far sea garden
and I smooth the slick white pages
in your dog-eared book

and I write: "Not your light, but snow . . ."

And then the long murmuring wind.
And then the bluebird at the window.

Small as Rain

Snow small as rain
wanders past the dark firs
and pines, barely touches
me. So slow this waking,
this waiting. The first threads
of grass unravel beneath
tiny corridors of stone
and the cold wedges of earth
left by elk and deer hooves
and the hooves of the black cows
sold this winter that will
not lay their calves down
again to sleep. This winter,
I snowshoed through wind-
carved shadows of blue trees,
drove past glittering ice rivers,
past wild geese quiet
on wet stones, deer
in the road ditches frost-
feathered, unafraid.
Soon, the gold banner
and the purple iris shall
riddle these fields, and the pink
geraniums rise,
and the boulder raspberry
float from winter dark
crevices through deep woods
and wild gardens, white
as the snow when we could touch
anyone.

To A Friend Wanting Beauty on Earth Day

I watched a video of an octopus
sleeping in a tank last night.
"Dreaming," the narrator said,
its ivory mantle dipping
beneath the black-lit water
like a soft bag I could touch.
Or a cow's nose, I kept thinking,
like the cows I've watched
half-dozing in yellow ponds
of light, the whole weight
of cows folded into the hot musk
of fields, our births and these deaths
just motes and summer dust
to them in their long grazing,
in the evening's coolness,
in the roots and weeds they touch.
But I walked down to these woods
to find something beautiful
for you, brushing these splinters
and green needles from this old log
so I could sit just
below the cusp of a winter
wind too long cold.
The air riffled through the pines—
a sea-murmur—and the white
octopus still dreamed, still
flushed gold, then coral.
Then, in the waking grass,
a chickadee strayed, the sky
a perfect pewter bowl,
and a flicker
at a hollow tree knocking
not ten feet away.

On Your Nightly Waking

That goddess blind,
That stands upon the rolling restless stone—
          Henry V, Act 3 Scene VI Shakespeare

I thought you still slept
beside me, suspended
above the spotted knapweed
I unwittingly let
grow in our fields, its purple
cloud invasive, I've been told,
though I've watched it suckled
by a thousand bees and painted
ladies, while the flame
of its witch's root burned
the other wildflowers out.
But I found you at the window,
beneath the Milky Way's rift,
naming the last few stars
hued in that Indian yellow
or what Van Gogh painted
his stars into soul with.
Hearing something, you asked,
What is this? and I said,
coyote or trickster, not
knowing yet how fate or chance
works, but only you,
faintest, creaking the stairs
how many times at night
to bend in pain alone,
to open the door in hope
of seeing elk at the peak
of rut, light-hastened
and dark-pinned, at the broken fence
we've yet to mend.

Bluebirds in April on My Birthday

Bluebirds tapped at the window
and I remembered years past
their eggs we found
blue as glass stones.
I fear the pink anemones
I seeded this spring will fray
by summer. Still, the birds
plow through the trees
in their winter dark coats.
I am stranded by walls
and masks I cup my mouth with.
"What child can ever again
blow out a candle?" a mother asks.
The bluebirds keep quilting
the abandoned cavities
of tree knots and the frayed
cowls of last year's nests
whole again. I did not know
there would be an old world
to miss at sixty-one.

Four Flickers in Flight

—HJ Burt, 1929-2020

That morning the flickers drilled
into tin, into aluminum
until we could not hear
the owls or the mourning doves
or the breath of each other,
you, love, finally lifted
a corner of our night blankets
and stepped into the early shadows
to unpin the window screens
and wave off the flickers
you love, their underwings
bright embers I could not see.
Now, I have looked at these flickers
so long, this spring with its griefs
I cannot unloosen
like the dark ice of the frozen
troughs I once filled
with a hose for my mother when I
was just a girl lonely in an Ohio winter
so cold that this ice I keep
carrying should break beneath
my hands, beneath these heavy
pine boughs I bend
beneath this morning, but
it doesn't. The flickers hammered
the gutters when I was young
and then when our own children
slept down dark hallways.
In this country of absence, my quiet,
blind mother still rocks
in the window blur of a yellow
rented room in a nursing
home where once I could enter
to touch her, my tongue speaking
like the far bell of a country
church she could still remember,
swaying in the air she cupped
her hands to catch.

Writing a Poem after My Mother Tells Me a Story

My mother told me about
a monkey chained to a cage
by a bar by a river by a bike
trail above the old train
tracks she once biked.
She said how sad it made her,
the monkey drinking from old
beer cans, chained
by his neck. I sit beneath
a lamp tonight, outside,
a railing, a ghost of trees.
In the morning, I'll hear roosters
and one dog barking
and elk will swell along the gully,
over the barbed wire fence
where brown and white horses
wander. I am trying to think
of a word to tell my mother
for what's outside this window,
not of the dark she already
knows nor night nor how
the sky blushes over Grouse
Mountain. On Fridays,
my mother would cry
in the shade of my front porch
in the suburbs where my poppies were still
a mound of green and my tulips
red-rose and half-
torn in the sprinkler's rain.
She wanted to die but we
would eat our favorite ice cream.
And now I sit here,
Venus tucked above a hem
of dark cloud,
and this desk lamp floating.

On Learning You Had Healed

We drove past a shining river,
a deer half-poised to flight
in a roadside ditch.
We drove until the sun scooped
down through the windshield
and blinded my right eye,
the mountain goats on Rainbow
Pass like sudden snow.
Finally arrived, here
at this cabin we made, I
was a snag of wood; I
was a fencepost, a red
glacier rock humbled
by the sky, bird-perched
and counting the shadows the wind
strewn across our porch steps,
your rocker anchored by a stone
of white quartz I pulled
for luck from a plowed road.
It was the morning I began
to call this cabin home,
to sit quiet in a cape
of sun where the spring trees
dappled it, where it drew
wild and full blossomed
across your night-worn body.
Quiet, I said, *quiet*,
the ground not shadow-
spun, the birds not dark.

Three Ravens Brush the Sky

I kneel in the dirt, in the still
wet winter, dig
my holes for the bulbs of these
tall stalked gladiolas
I am already dreaming
into pink and silk mouths.
I like to think Eve
did it, a story from a faith
not mine, as if our Eve
fell here, burrowing
deep into this dirt to go home,
so lost her garden, so
dark this dirt with its old
leaves and frost burn
and its unnamed galaxies
of vole bones and the field mice
 my neighbor keeps trapping
in the meadows by his trailer.
Sixty-three in an afternoon,
he tells me. Cold April,
I watch the ravens buck,
then skid down the west
wind past the homestead
barn, past the black
mud of a spring I have stepped
so many times through
to linger at its empty windows
where once a family milked
a hundred dairy cows,
carried the milk to a train along
the tracks to an old gold
mine where the burros the miners
left behind in the tallow
dark of candles are just bones.

Now, a butterfly floats beside me,
small in the wind
where it climbed wet-winged
from a white cocoon
to flicker above the purple

knapweed that will rise
from the late summer dirt.
Still the ravens keep flying,
each a black scrawl
in a wind that hurls past
Bull Mountain over still
yellow meadows and ponds
washed blue in the sun,
nothing, I think, to leave now,

nothing.

To the Swallow This Spring at the Nest Box

I own nothing of you
nor this leaf that shivers
into a half-bud above
the phlox and blue flax
that burrow with me
into this old winter grass.
Yet how much I yearn
for your blue-struck wing
like an arrow over a sun-
struck river, as if it were some
prayer to fit between
my strange and lonely palm,
so hollow its feathers,
so frail I think I could breathe
through them, so iridescent the sky
you harbor down that
whoever hammered this wood
together did so
in such hurry, in such
love, they left even
the nails unflattened. And now
your nestling waits
at this world someone
cored into the box for it
to see: a little
knot of light,
a song
to dip and break against.

Sitting on a Bench My Father Sat On

I press my back hard
against the bench to feel
what my dying father felt
sick and lost so long ago
in some dream, some blur, some river
glittering I have yet to see.
Twenty years ago,
he sat on this bench by a man-made
pond in Ohio, blue green
from the copper sulfate he used
to clean it. Here on its perch
of rocks where I carried it,
the lightest flecks of aspen,
the blue-wash of the Arkansas Valley,
the tinder of snow on Green Mountain
surround me. What would my doctor
father say, sitting
in this cacophony of bird song,
its tin and chime, bell
and croak in this world of no touch?
The spring wind swirls
through the crevices,
the understory of these woods.
The green haze buds, and flickers
weave through the arms of the dark pine,
the neighbor's rooster half-crowing
at me above the gully.
Soon enough, I'll find
littered beneath the cabin porch
the stems of the white flowers
in a blue vase I drove up
from the suburbs to lean against
this sun-warmed wood.
The dog noses me twice,
and a fly settles on my keyboard, surfs
across its metal light.

Morning on the Cabin Porch

The humming bird mistakes
me for a flower: something
half-wan and camouflaged
in a wild iris shirt.
The aspens riddle my slant
of sun like snakes of shade.
Far off, past the pines,
a meadow lark trills
from the draw where, yesterday,
I found bear scat fresh,
flies swarming it.
I walked, clapping my hands
at the dark of woods until they hurt.
Now the air stirs.
A hummingbird zips
past the porch, circles,
hovers, a tiny god at my face.
I am all blossom and sepal,
sweet petal and wing dust.
And at my feet, a tiny bee
crawls for the first time.

The Sky A Wild Creature

by this time we are both an open secret —*James Wright*

I dried the last pan,
let it clatter onto the shelf
beneath the oven, still warm
from our chicken and sweet potatoes.
You had hurt yourself again,
the tender threads of your knees
torn I feared. I didn't say anything,
silence these days a companion
of the house like the field mouse
we can't find in the shed
that shreds through the new bags
of oiled sunflower seeds
you drive up from the plains,
their husks like scattered boats.
To see the pink moon, I told you,
then unhooked the crooked latch
and walked out into the cold.
The wind wound itself
around me, lifted my hair,
touched my face. I placed
my feet like loaves of bread
in the snow thaw, a piping
of hidden birds the whole
time I walked. The moon
was chalk, the moon was
a stone statue, a face cratered,
a doorway of light, everything
I'd ever heard of. And the old grass
was the color of wild mustard,
and the new grass, shredded
by the neighbor's plow all winter,
mute and dark-winged.

I wondered why it mattered
to me, thirteen full moons
this year, moons named *Wolf*
or *Snow* or *Worm* before we even
settled indoors this moment
to live separate from everyone
else we knew. The angus
cows were nowhere, feeding
elsewhere on scraps of winter
grass. I missed their breathing,
their heads swinging from their necks
thick as obsidian, totems
or sentries watching me
pass in peace. The wind
knocked me down the lane,
a slab of wind until I curved
south, moon at my shoulder.
I wanted this to be beautiful;
I wanted this to be about love,
even the bluebirds plowing the air.
I kept watching the moon,
thinking it pink, thinking
this will never be again,
this new world awful
and frightening, and you, love,
quiet in the loft, waiting
for me. Then, the moon lifted
my shadow like a feather, and a bird
I startled from the bunched grass
carved itself into an arrow,
the sky a wild creature.

Notes

pg 1: Sirius is known as the Dog Star because it is part of Canis Major, or the Big Dog. The ancient Egyptians linked it with the goddess Isis, a goddess of healing and magic who the later Romans associated with Fate; *The Rosicrucian Egyptian Museum.*

pg. 2: The first full moon of April, the Pink Moon is named for the bloom of pink phlox, *The Old Farmer's Almanac.* 1800 dead in the United States through Covid was reported the night of the Pink Moon.

pg. 5: Divination, Augury is the divination of the future through the observation of natural phenomena, particularly in the movement of birds. *Britannica.*

pg. 7: Zeus named the Iris flower after the goddess of rainbows. *Gods and Goddesses Associated with Plants*, www.nps.gov.

pg. 7: The Pasque Flower, also known as the Easter flower and the Wind flower, is named for the time it blooms, near Easter. Legends associate it with sorrow and pain. *Rocky Mountain Wildflowers* by Jerry Pavia.

pg. 8: Mt. Vesuvius erupted in 70 A.D. Pliny the Younger at the time was a young man who watched his Uncle, Pliny the Elder, sail across the Bay of Naples to help those trapped by the burning ash and lava. Pliny the Elder succumbed to the fumes of the volcano, along with those who were affixiated and burned to death in Pompei. Casts of their bodies left in the cooled lava; Institute of Geophysics and Planetary Physics, University of California: San Diego.

pg. 10: Hanami is a Japanese tradition of savoring the beauty of the transient flower, particularly the cherry blossom. *Japan Experience.*

pg. 13: Blue Harebell is associated, among other things, with grief. artofmourning.com pg. 17: The Goddess of Chance or Fate in Roman times, Fortunae, was thought to stand blindfolded, a symbol of her blindness, upon the wheel of fortune. *Britannica.* She is described in Shakespeare's play, *Henry V* Act III Scene VI.

pg. 22: According to Jewish folktale, Lilith was the first wife to Adam, who, discontented, left the Garden on her own, only to return later to discover that Eve had replaced her; Department of Religious Studies, Kenyon College.

Kathryn Winograd, poet, essayist, and writer@9600ft, is the author of six books, including her most recent collection of essays, *Slow Arrow: Unearthing the Frail Children*, which received a Bronze Medal in Essay for the 2020 Independent Publisher Book Awards and is Foreword INDIES Book of the Year Awards Finalist. Her first collection, *Phantom Canyon: Essays of Reclamation*, was also a Foreword INDIES Finalist. *Air Into Breath*, her first book of poetry, an alternate for the Yale Series for Younger Poets, was a Colorado Book Award Winner.

Her essays have been noted in *Best American Essays,* and published in journals and anthologies including *Arts & Letters, Fourth Genre, Hotel Amerika, River Teeth, The Florida Review, Essay Daily, and The Fourth Genre: Contemporary Writers of/on Creative Nonfiction, 6th edition.*

Her poetry has received three Pushcart Prize nominations and a Special Mention in Pushcart Prize XXXVIII. Poems have won the *Chautauqua Literary Journal*'s Poetry contest on War and Peace and the *Writers Digest* Annual Writing Competition for non-rhyming poetry. Her poetry has appeared over the years in numerous literary journals, as diverse as *The New Yorker* and *Cricket Magazine for Children.*

Winograd has been a longtime educator and arts advocate, teaching creative writing for over 35 years to writers of all ages and experience. She taught poetry and creative nonfiction for Ashland University's low residency MFA program for ten years and currently teaches for Regis University's Mile High MFA. She holds a Ph.D. in Literature and Creative Writing from the University of Denver and an MFA in poetry from the University of Iowa.

www.ingramcontent.com/pod-product-compliance
Lightning Source LLC
Chambersburg PA
CBHW030459100426
42813CB00002B/281